ANCIENT MACHINES

ANCIENT TECHNOLOGY

ANCIENT MACHINES

FROM WEDGES TO WATERWHEELS

by Michael Woods
and
Mary B. Woods

 RUNESTONE PRESS • MINNEAPOLIS

A DIVISION OF LERNER PUBLISHING GROUP

*Dedicated to school librarians, teachers, moms and dads,
and others who help kids read*

Series designer: Zachary Marell
Series editors: Joelle E. Riley and Dina Drits
Copy editor: Margaret J. Goldstein
Photograph researcher: Dan Mahoney

Runestone Press
A Division of Lerner Publishing Group
241 First Avenue North
Minneapolis, MN 55401 U.S.A.

Website address: www.lernerbooks.com

LIBRARY OF CONGRESS CATALOGING-IN-PUBLICATION DATA

Woods, Michael, 1946–
      Ancient machines: from wedges to waterwheels / Michael and
Mary B. Woods.
        p. cm. — (Ancient technology)
      Includes bibliographical references and index.
      Summary: Discusses the invention of six simple machines in
various ancient civilizations from the Stone Age to the fall of the
Roman Empire.
      ISBN 0–8225–2994–7 (alk. paper)
      1. Simple machines—Juvenile literature. 2. Machinery—History—
Juvenile literature. [1. Simple machines. 2. Machinery—History.]
I. Woods, Mary B. (Mary Boyle), 1946– . II. Title. III. Series.
TJ147.w66 2000
621.8—dc21   98–30289

Manufactured in the United States of America
1 2 3 4 5 6 – AM – 05 04 03 02 01 00

TABLE OF CONTENTS

What do you think of when you hear the word *technology*? You probably think of something totally new. You might think of research laboratories filled with computers, powerful microscopes, and other scientific tools. But technology doesn't refer only to brand-new machines and discoveries. Technology is as old as human society.

Technology is the use of knowledge, inventions, and discoveries to make human life better. The word *technology* comes from two Greek words. One, *tekhne*, means "art" or "craft." The other, *logia*, means "reason" or "logic." The ancient Greeks originally used the word *technology* to mean a discussion of arts and crafts. But, in modern times, *technology* usually refers to a craft, technique, or tool itself.

People use many kinds of technology. Medicine is one kind of technology. Transportation and agriculture are also kinds of technology. These technologies and many others help make human life easier, safer, and more enjoyable. This book takes a look at another important kind of technology—one that has helped human life tremendously. That technology is machinery.

SIMPLE AND COMPLEX

A machine is a device that does work. You know what work means. Work usually involves doing or making something—accomplishing a task. But engineers have a special definition of work. To engineers, work means transferring energy from one object to another. This transfer of energy causes the object to move or change direction. When an engine moves an automobile, for instance, the engine is doing work. When you turn the pages of this book, you are doing work. The amount of work that is done depends on the amount of force applied to the object. Force means push or pull.

Machines allow people to apply more force and do more work than could be done with muscle power alone. With machines, force can also be applied more efficiently.

Some machines have hundreds of moving parts and are powered by motors. Other machines are very basic. Scissors, tweezers, knives, and bottle openers are not complicated. They do not have ball bearings, pistons, gears, or valves. They do not burn fuel. They are easy to use. Yet they are machines.

ANCIENT ROOTS

All machines, no matter how complicated they seem, are based on some combination of only six simple machines. The simple machines are the lever, the wheel and axle, the inclined plane, the pulley, the wedge, and the screw. They were all developed in ancient times. Combinations of simple machines are used to make complex machines.

You've probably heard people remark, "There's nothing new under the sun!" That's especially true when

NORTH
AMERICA

Atlantic
Ocean

Pacific
Ocean

N

SOUTH
AMERICA

CIVILIZATIONS OF THE
Ancient World
(through A.D. 476)

EUROPE

ASIA

AFRICA

Indian
Ocean

6000 B.C. ————————————— 534 B.C.		Middle East
3100 B.C. ———————————— 30 B.C.		Egypt
1766 B.C. ————————————		China
1200 B.C. ————————————		Mesoamerica
800 B.C. ———————— 146 B.C.		Greece
509 B.C. ——————— A.D. 476		Rome
320 B.C. ———————		India

Stone Age civilizations have flourished in
most parts of the world. These cultures began and
ended at different times in different regions.

we're talking about machines. An ancient Greek or Roman engineer, somehow transported to modern times, would marvel at automobile engines, construction cranes, nuclear power plants, and assembly lines. But this engineer might also be amazed at how little some basic machine technology has changed over the centuries.

Modern engineers have improved on ancient ideas. They have found new ways to assemble simple machines into complex ones. They have developed lubricants that make machines more efficient. They have learned to make machines faster, more precise, more powerful, and more durable. But modern people still rely on the six simple machines in building new machines.

Historians use the word *ancient* to refer to the period from the first human societies to the fall of the Western Roman Empire in A.D. 476. The first humans lived about 2.5 million years ago.

Historians divide ancient history into three ages, or periods, based on the main materials that people used to make machines. The first period was the Stone Age, when people made tools mostly from stone (though they also used wood, bone, and other materials). The Stone Age was followed by the Bronze Age and the Iron Age. These periods occurred at different times in different parts of the world.

In this book, you'll learn about wedges that could split giant walls of stone, and about the Claws of Archimedes, which could lift whole battleships out of the water and smash them to pieces. Read on to find out about these devices and others that are sure to amaze you.

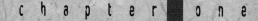

THE STONE AGE

Cave painting of cattle and people from
Tassili N'Ajjer in Algeria

The earliest era of human history was the Stone Age. Stone Age people were hunters and gatherers. They lived by fishing, catching game, and gathering edible wild plants. After eating all the food in one area, people would move to another place to find new food supplies. Sometimes Stone Age people followed herds of wild animals, which were also a source of food.

Stone Age people used many tools to help them with daily activities such as gathering food. These tools included levers, knives, and bows.

THE LEVER

The lever, the simplest of all machines, was a common tool in the Stone Age. A lever is a bar or beam used to lift objects or pry them loose. When Stone Age people used sticks to pry rocks and edible roots from the ground, these sticks became levers.

With the earliest type of lever, if a person pushed down on one end of it, the person

13

could lift a load, such as a rock, with the other end of the lever. As it operated, the lever pivoted, or turned, against a support called a fulcrum. The first fulcrum was probably the ground itself. But people gradually realized that it was easier to pry with a lever if they could use a rock or piece of wood as a fulcrum.

Stone Age people used oars and paddles, which are also levers, to propel rafts and small boats. The bracket for holding an oar against the side of a boat was the fulcrum. The person paddling supplied the force, in the form of muscle power.

THE WEDGE

Stone Age people used yet another simple machine, the wedge. A wedge is a piece of wood, metal, or other material that is thicker at one end than at the other. Wedges are used to move loads a short distance. Nails, knives, axes, and chisels are all kinds of wedges. Our front teeth even work as wedges.

Imagine cutting an apple with a knife. The tip of the knife, the thinnest edge, begins to split the apple. As the knife moves deeper into the apple, the wider edge splits the apple even more. Likewise, the pointed tip of a nail acts as a wedge that separates the fibers of wood, gradually moving them farther apart as the nail goes deeper into the wood.

Stone Age people used stone wedges and axes to split logs. They probably drove wedges into cracks in the logs using rocks and hammers. Stone Age people also used razor-sharp stone knives to butcher mammoths and other large animals. Some of the oldest known tools are stone

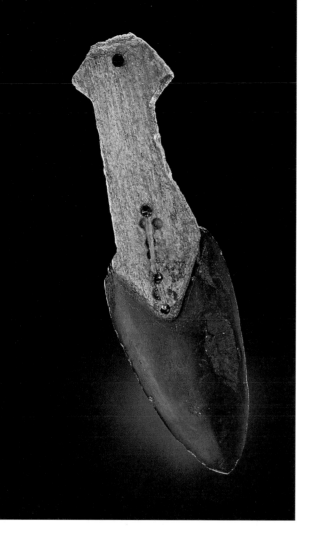

Slate-bladed knife with bone handle found on Baffin Island, Canada

knives and axes found in the Omo River Valley in the modern country of Ethiopia. These tools are estimated to be around two million years old.

THE BOW

The bow was another Stone Age machine. The Stone Age bow was a long strip of wood connected at both ends by a vine or string of animal hide or tendon. Archaeologists, scientists who study the remains of past cultures, don't know when the bow was developed. Many archaeologists think the device was first used more than thirty thousand years ago in parts of North Africa.

When we think of bows, we often think of a bow and arrow, used as a weapon. But the first bows were probably not used as weapons. They were used as drills.

Here's how the bow drill works: the bowstring is looped around the pointed shaft, which consists of a long, narrow stick or stone. By moving the bow in a sawing, or back-and-forth, motion, a person can set the shaft spinning. The point of the shaft is then used to drill holes in wood. The tip acts like a wedge—opening up a hole in the material. Although a bow drill does not look like a wheel, it functions on the principle of the wheel and axle, one of the six simple machines. The drill shaft acts as an axle. The string's rotational movement around the shaft describes the shape of a circle, just like the rim of a wheel.

The bow drill's movement creates friction, which occurs when objects rub together. Friction slows down moving objects. You can experience friction yourself by pressing the palms of your hands together and rubbing rapidly. Notice how the rubbing motion slows your hands a little. Do you also notice a warm feeling when you rub? Friction creates heat.

The bow drill's friction loosens small particles of the substance being drilled, producing a hole. If the hole is being drilled into wood, the heat created by friction also burns the wood, so the hole is cut faster. Bow drills can actually start fires when spun rapidly in a pile of dry leaves or wood chips.

Stone Age people may have even used the bow drill to perform brain surgery! Archaeologists think that Stone Age

An Inuit man in northern Canada drills bone with a bow drill.

surgeons cut holes in the skulls of sick people to release "evil spirits" from their head. Hundreds of Stone Age skulls show signs of this procedure.

BOWS AND ARROWS

Bows, when used with arrows, also served as weapons in ancient times. People began using bows and arrows as weapons around 16,000 B.C. The Egyptians hunted with bows and arrows, and used them in wars against the Persians, who fought with only slingshots and spears.

Crossbows, developed in China in the fourth century B.C., had more power than ordinary bows. The crossbow had a crank or lever for drawing back the string and arrow. The arrow could be held in a cocked position for as long as needed.

In ancient Greece and Rome, engineers took the bow and arrow concept one step further. They made big catapults that were like giant bows cocked with tense springs. Catapults shot large arrows and stones, much farther and with more accuracy than ordinary bows.

All of these weapons were based on principles of simple machines. In a longbow, for instance, the archer's hand acted like the fulcrum on a lever. The bow rotated around the fulcrum. Crossbows used cranks and pulleys that also were simple machines.

2

ANCIENT MIDDLE EAST

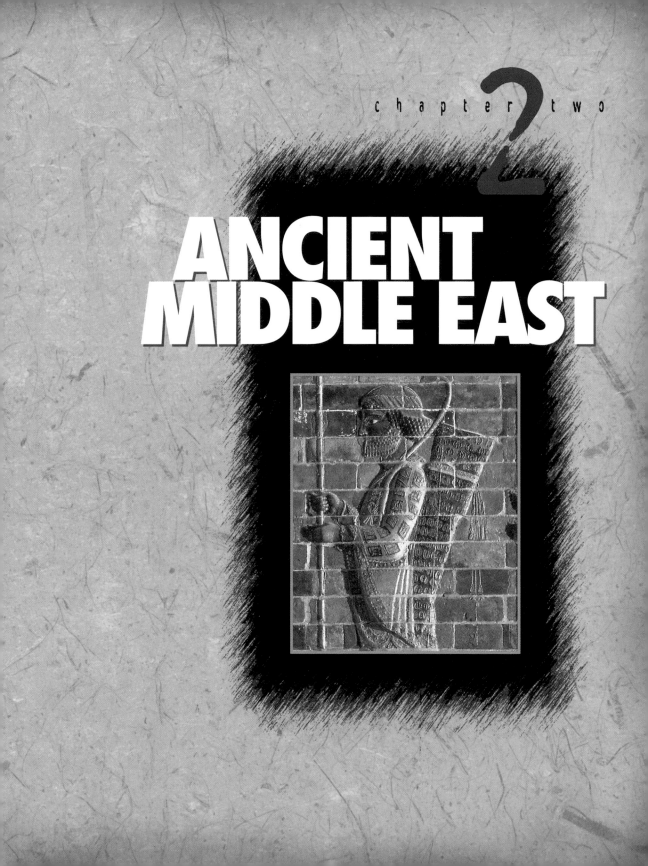

Frieze of Persian king Darius's archer
guards, made around 500 B.C.

Beginning around 10,000 B.C., people in the Middle East—the region where Asia, Africa, and Europe meet—began to abandon the hunter-gatherer lifestyle. They settled in the Fertile Crescent, an arc of fertile land extending from the eastern Mediterranean Sea to the Persian Gulf.

Some people settled between the Tigris and Euphrates Rivers, in what has since become Iraq. The Greeks later named this region Mesopotamia, which means "between rivers." One group settled in Sumer, in southern Mesopotamia, and established the first great civilization in the Fertile Crescent. The Sumerians grew grain, vegetables, and fruit. They domesticated, or tamed, wild animals. They settled into permanent farming villages. Other groups in the ancient Middle East included the Babylonians, Hittites, and Assyrians.

Some of our most important machines originated in the ancient Middle East. These include the pulley and the wheel and axle. People in the

Middle East also began to use new materials, such as copper and bronze, to make stronger and more durable machines. The Hittites were among the first people to make iron.

THE PULLEY

Which is easier—using your body weight to pull down on an object, or lifting it upward? If you've ever used a pulley to raise a bucket from an old well, for instance, you know how your body weight can help you lift a load.

A pulley is a wheel with a grooved rim. Here's how it works: imagine a tall pole with a pulley on top and a rope passing over the groove in the pulley and hanging down to the ground at both ends. If you attach a load to one end of the rope, you can lift it by pulling on the other end.

The first pulleys were probably used to hoist buckets of water. The first known picture of a pulley appears in a battle scene that was drawn in ancient Assyria during the eighth century B.C. The picture shows a bearded warrior holding a bucket that had been hoisted over the walls of a fort with a pulley.

At first, the Assyrians used a fixed pulley, like the pulley at the top of a flagpole. This machine didn't increase the force of a person's pull. It simply changed the direction of force—a person pulling downward could lift loads upward.

Another basic type of pulley was the movable pulley. A load was attached to one end of the pulley and a rope was passed through the groove of the pulley. One end of the rope was attached to a fixed support above the load (for example, a hook on a ceiling) and a person pulled up on the other end.

Later, people learned to combine a fixed pulley with

movable pulleys to make what is called a compound pulley, or block and tackle. A block is a unit of one or more pulleys working together. A tackle is a rope that passes over the groove in a pulley. In a compound pulley, one pulley is attached to a fixed support, such as a strong hook in an overhead beam. This pulley changes the direction of force. Other pulleys are attached to the load or to ropes and move freely. These movable pulleys multiply the force of a person's pull, reducing the force needed to lift a load.

Each movable pulley in a compound pulley reduces the force needed to lift a load. If one movable pulley is used, the effort needed is divided by two. In a block with five movable pulleys, the effort needed is divided by six.

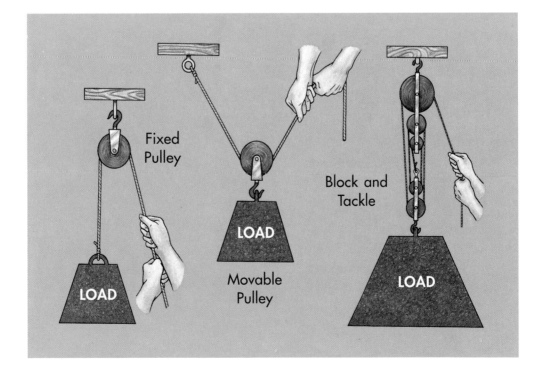

Fixed Pulley

Movable Pulley

Block and Tackle

LOAD

LOAD

LOAD

Some experts trace the compound pulley to Archimedes, a Greek engineer and mathematician who lived from 287 to 212 B.C. One story tells how Archimedes used a series of compound pulleys to single-handedly launch a ship, pulling it from a dry dock into the ocean.

THE WHEEL AND AXLE

The Assyrians used another of the six simple machines, the wheel and axle. Mention wheels and most people think of round devices that help cars, bicycles, and other vehicles roll along roads. Most people think of an axle as the shaft attached to the center of a wheel.

To engineers, the wheel and axle aren't just devices for helping vehicles move. A wheel and axle work together as one machine to increase (or sometimes to reduce) force. The wheel and axle are actually two different wheels, one bigger than the other. The axle is usually smaller than the wheel, but not always. In machines, force applied to the wheel turns the axle.

Many modern devices are based on the wheel and axle. These include doorknobs, wrenches, screwdrivers, steering wheels, and water faucets. Did you ever try to turn a water faucet that was missing its handle? It is almost impossible to turn the slender stem (the axle). But the faucet's larger handle (the wheel) turns easily, because large wheels increase force more than small wheels. The easy-to-turn handle is attached to the hard-to-turn stem and moves it with much less force than is needed to turn the stem alone.

The ancient Assyrians used the wheel and axle in a device called a windlass, or winch. It had a cranklike handle (the wheel) connected to a center axle and a length of rope. When the crank was turned, rope wrapped around the axle, hoisting an object attached to the rope. The Assyrians probably used the windlass to lift water from wells, and dirt and metal from mines.

SPINNING

Ancient people began domesticating sheep about 11,000 years ago. Sheep provided milk and meat for food, and wool to make cloth. Before wool and other types of fiber could be woven into cloth, however, they had to be prepared for weaving by a process called spinning.

Most natural fibers are very short. Cotton fibers, for instance, are only about half an inch long. Spinning changes short pieces of wool, cotton, or other fibers into long strands of thread or yarn, which can then be woven.

Mesopotamians used machines called the spindle and the distaff to spin wool by hand. The distaff was a small stick with a slot on one end to hold clumps of wool. The spindle was a straight stick held between thumb and finger. By twirling the spindle, a person could carefully draw fibers off of the distaff. The short wool fibers clung and twisted together, creating a long thread or strand.

People learned to maintain the momentum, or continuous motion, of the spindle by attaching it to a small clay disk called a whorl. The whorl was one of the earliest flywheels. A flywheel is a heavy wheel attached to a shaft. It is able to store up energy and then release it to give a machine the momentum to keep rotating at a constant speed.

The whorl led to the development of a spinning wheel—a bigger wheel operated by a foot pedal. Like the smaller whorl, the spinning wheel moved at a constant speed and

Four-thousand-year-old whorl

kept even tension on the thread or yarn. This tension assured a smooth, uniform strand.

Archaeologists believe that the spinning wheel was first developed in ancient India around 500 B.C. The basic design of the spinning wheel has not changed since ancient times.

BETTER MATERIALS

The first machines were built mainly from stone, wood, and vines, and from animal bone, hair, and hide. Ancient people knew how to best use these materials. They knew that willow branches bend easily, so these can be curved to make handles and baskets. Cedar wood resists decay when wet, so it was used to build ships. Hickory and ash don't split easily. So these woods made good wheels and tool handles. Oak is extremely strong and was used to make levers and wedges.

Ancient people eventually discovered other materials that could make their machines even more powerful and more efficient. These materials were metals. Metals have great advantages over stone, bone, and wood. Metals are stronger and last longer, of course. But they also have a property called plasticity, which means they can be melted, bent, stretched, shaped, and reshaped. Plasticity is very important to machine makers.

Ancient people used gold and copper in toolmaking as early as 8,000 B.C. Imagine an ancient toolmaker striking a lump of gold or copper and discovering that it could be bent and beaten into many different shapes. How amazing these metals must have seemed! No wonder ancient people regarded gold and copper as magical and valuable.

COPPER

Extracting metal from the earth was not easy. Ancient craftspeople who wanted to make a tool out of copper couldn't just pick up a big lump of copper from a mine. Instead, they might find that copper was combined with other substances inside a blue-green rock called malachite. To get the copper, ancient craftspeople had to remove it from the malachite.

A rock (such as malachite) that contains a valuable metal (such as copper) is called an ore. Separating metal from its ore involves a process called smelting.

The process requires high temperatures. Ancient people probably smelted metal in ovens or pottery kilns. Science historians think that copper was the first metal to be smelted from its ore in large amounts.

Copper was first smelted in ancient Thailand and later in Mesopotamia. By 2600 B.C., copper-making technology had spread to Egypt, where copper was used in machines,

Bronze ax heads made around 1800 B.C., found in present-day Iran

weapons, and other products. Much of Egypt's copper came from mines on the island of Cyprus. Our modern word *copper* comes from the ancient word for Cyprus.

STRONGER METALS

The next era in toolmaking technology was the Bronze Age. Archaeologists originally thought the Bronze Age began in the ancient Middle East. But new evidence suggests that the Bronze Age actually began around 4500 B.C. in Thailand. Bronze ages occurred at other times in other areas—in Greece about 3000 B.C., in China around 1800 B.C., and in the Americas about A.D. 1000.

Bronze is an alloy, or mixture, of copper and other metals. The first bronzes were alloys of copper and tin. Ancient craftspeople found that bronze was harder, stronger, and more durable than pure copper. They also found that bronze could be easily cast: melted into liquid, poured into molds, and hardened. A broken bronze tool could easily be melted and recast into another tool or weapon. Bronze was the main metal used for tools, weapons, and armor in the Mediterranean world for several thousand years.

In about 1200 B.C., ancient people began to make tools from an even stronger metal, iron. The Hittites were among the first people to use iron. Their iron spears and battle axes gave them an advantage over enemies who used softer bronze weapons.

Though iron was stronger than bronze, it was harder to make into tools. Ancient furnaces could not reach temperatures high enough to melt iron into liquid. (Iron melts at about 2800 degrees Fahrenheit.) So there was only one way to shape iron into objects. Red-hot iron had to be pulled from the furnace and pounded into shape with a heavy hammer. Iron that is shaped by pounding instead of casting is called wrought iron. Centuries after people began using iron, people in China discovered ways of casting it.

The next metal ancient people used was steeled iron, which we call steel. Steel is iron with extra carbon in it. The extra carbon makes steel stronger and more durable than ordinary iron. Some experts think that ancient blacksmiths accidentally produced steel by heating iron tools in beds of charcoal. The tools absorbed carbon from the charcoal and became stronger. Archaeologists believe that by the tenth century B.C., blacksmiths were intentionally steeling iron by heating iron and charcoal together.

THE FIRST MACHINE TOOL

Ancient machine-building technology went beyond the use of hand tools such as knives and hammers. Machine tools are the basis of modern industry. They are usually large, power-driven tools used for cutting, forming, and shaping metal, wood, and plastic. Machine tools are often used to make other tools.

Many textbooks say that an Englishman named John Wilkinson invented the first machine tool in A.D. 1775. It was a boring machine, used to drill holes in metal. But experts know that the first machine tool was really made more than three thousand years earlier. It was the lathe.

A lathe is a machine tool used to shape wood, metal, or other material. The material to be shaped, called a workpiece, is cut into shape as it rotates against the lathe's sharp blade. Lathes are often used to carve decorative, rounded wooden legs for chairs and other furniture.

Twenty-five-hundred-year-old wall relief of King Darius of Persia sitting on a throne. The throne's legs were probably turned on a lathe.

Pictures from the ancient Middle East, some dating to 1500 B.C., show furniture and other objects that clearly were turned, or cut, with a lathe. One picture shows a Persian king, Darius, sitting on a throne that has turned legs. Darius lived from 550 to 486 B.C.

The first lathes were operated by foot pedals. Archaeologists believe that Greek traders saw lathes in the Middle East and introduced them to Europe in the seventh century B.C.

ANCIENT EGYPT

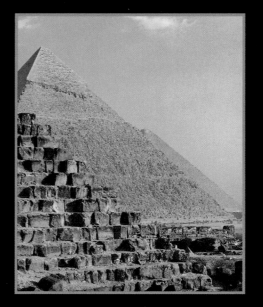

Ancient Egypt is probably most famous for its giant pyramids, which were tombs for its rulers, called pharaohs. Not only do the pyramids serve as lasting memorials to the pharaohs, they also attest to the great knowledge and skill of Egyptian architects and engineers.

Egypt's largest pyramid, the Great Pyramid, is the tomb of Pharaoh Khufu. It was built at Giza around 2600 B.C. The Great Pyramid is 481 feet high. Each side of its base is 756 feet long—the length of more than two and a half football fields. Builders used two million blocks of limestone to make the pyramid. Most blocks weighed about 3.5 tons (seven thousand pounds) apiece.

The Egyptians used some simple machines in their building. They used the lever, the inclined plane, and the wedge. An inclined plane is a flat surface that slopes up and down. It sounds so simple that it might be hard to believe an inclined plane is really a machine. But, in fact,

35

the inclined plane is one of the most important machines there is for moving heavy loads to a higher level.

Although the Egyptians knew about the lever, the inclined plane, and the wedge, they didn't know about the pulley, the wheel and axle, and the screw at the time of the pyramids. How did the Egyptians build the pyramids with so few tools? How did the workers raise such heavy blocks into position as a pyramid rose hundreds of feet above the ground?

ONE THEORY

The Greek historian Herodotus, who lived from 484 B.C. to 425 B.C., is one of our best sources of information about life in ancient Egypt. He tells us that a hundred thousand men worked for 20 years to build the Great Pyramid. According to Herodotus, the Egyptians used a series of levers to lift the giant limestone blocks into place. He describes the process:

> The pyramid was built in steps. . . . After laying the stones for the base, they raised the remaining stones to their places by means of machines formed of short wooden planks. The first machine raised them from the ground to the top of the first step. On this there was another machine, which received the stone upon its arrival, and conveyed it to the second step, whence a third machine advanced it still higher.

For centuries, people relied on Herodotus's description. Archaeologists searched for evidence that levers were used to lift the giant stone blocks from level to level on the pyramids.

They learned that the pyramid builders *did* use levers.

Workers levered blocks from rock quarries onto sledges (rectangular platforms used as vehicles) and river barges. Workers also used levers to position blocks at the pyramid site. But archaeologists have never found any evidence in Egyptian art or writing to show that the giant stone blocks were raised according to Herodotus's description.

Though Herodotus wrote that a hundred thousand men built the Great Pyramid over 20 years, some engineers think the tomb was built much more quickly with less manpower. The permanent barracks at the pyramid site would have housed a staff of only four thousand.

Herodotus is called "the Father of History," but it is important to remember that he wrote about events in Egypt about two thousand years after they happened. Any historian writing about events thousands of years before his or her time is bound to make some mistakes. Herodotus got his information as a tourist would. He visited Egypt and talked to the local people. His information was only as accurate as the stories he heard. But the stories may not have always been accurate.

If the Egyptians didn't use levers to lift blocks as they built the pyramids, what did they use? Archaeologists have found remains of earthen ramps at several pyramid sites. They think that builders used these ramps to move the blocks into position. As a pyramid rose higher, workers built the ramps higher. They hauled stones up the ramps on sledges, or rectangular platforms that can slide over many surfaces. Have you ever seen someone wheel a washing machine or refrigerator up a metal ramp or plank and into a truck? That plank is an inclined plane—one of the six simple machines.

Ramp from Abu Roash, an Egyptian pyramid site

MECHANICAL ADVANTAGE

Just how helpful is an inclined plane (or any other machine) to a person lifting a load? Engineers would answer that question by telling you about mechanical advantage. Mechanical advantage is the amount of help that a machine provides in doing work. For example, if a lever allows you to move a two-hundred-pound stone with just 50 pounds of force, then the lever has multiplied your force by four. So the mechanical advantage of that lever is four.

In the case of the inclined plane, mechanical advantage is equal to the length of the plane divided by the height the object must be raised. So if you needed to raise a refrigerator six feet into a truck, a six-foot ramp would be of little help. Its mechanical advantage (6 divided by 6) would be only one. With an 18-foot ramp, however, loading the refrigerator would be a breeze. The ramp's mechanical advantage (18 divided by 6) would be three: for every three pounds of load, the mover would need to exert only one pound of force.

The example shows that the longer the inclined plane, the more the mechanical advantage. The ancient Egyptians used ramps that were hundreds—even thousands—of feet long. This was the only way to gain the mechanical advantage needed to move giant stones to great heights.

WATER-POWERED WEDGES

Before the pyramid builders could begin their work, they had to remove stone from quarries. This was another major engineering project requiring thousands of laborers. One ancient writer told how Ramses II, who ruled Egypt from 1279 to 1212 B.C., sent an expedition of 9,000 people to a distant stone quarry. The group included 5,000 soldiers, 2,800 cooks, and 900 government officials. They were there to help 1 artist, 2 draftsmen, 3 master stonecutters, 4 sculptors, and 130 quarry workers.

Egyptian stonecutters had a clever way of splitting the large slabs. They inserted wooden wedges into natural cracks in the rock or into a line of drilled holes. Then they

The Industrial Revolution:
Why Not Earlier?

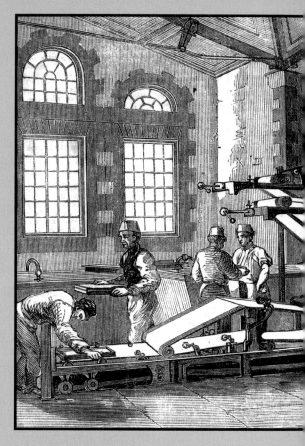

The Industrial Revolution started in England around A.D. 1750. It changed Europe from a farming society to one based on large-scale manufacturing. It involved many other changes, including migration of people from farms to cities. The Industrial Revolution occurred partly because people applied scientific and technological knowledge to manufacturing. Much of that knowledge was not new. It had been discovered in ancient times.

Experts sometimes wonder why an industrial revolution never occurred two thousand years earlier in ancient Greece or Rome. The Greeks and Romans had much of the mechanical knowledge needed for large-scale manufacturing. They even had a prime mover—a steam engine that was invented by a Greek named Hero of Alexandria. (The steam engine was an important part of the actual Industrial Revolution.)

Paper mill in A.D. 1854. The workers are making paper for bank notes.

Perhaps an industrial revolution never came about in ancient times because agricultural technology had not advanced far enough. During the A.D. 1700s and 1800s, people learned better ways to cultivate the land and to plant and harvest crops. Food production increased greatly. With a bigger food supply, population increased. There was a greater demand for clothing and other manufactured goods. Since farming had become more efficient, fewer people were needed to work the land and more were available to work in factories.

soaked the wedges with water. Wood swells and expands when wet. So the wedges expanded and enlarged the cracks in the rock. After about 10 hours, the stonecutters inserted larger wooden wedges and repeated the process until a slab of rock broke free. In a similar way, the ancient Greeks used cork wedges to split slabs of marble.

Who figured out how to cut giant stone slabs with wedges and move them great distances using levers and inclined planes? Perhaps it was Imhotep, chancellor, or secretary, to the pharaoh Zoser. Around 2650 B.C., Imhotep supervised construction of the Step Pyramid at Saqqara, the first pyramid built in Egypt.

An Egyptian priest and historian named Manetho called Imhotep the "inventor of the art of building in hewn stone." In addition to engineering, Imhotep practiced medicine. He was one of the ancient world's greatest physicians.

Everyday Machines

Egyptian engineers put their skills to work in more than just pyramid building. Many important household devices have origins in ancient Egypt. One is the clock.

Ancient people cared about time almost as much as modern people do. Priests had to make sacrifices at specific times of day. Soldiers needed to know when to perform their duties. In some ancient societies, lawyers and lawmakers were given time limits during debates.

The ancient Egyptians built the first clock around 1500 B.C. This was the clepsydra, a kind of water clock. It was a pottery jar with vertical markings on the inside and a small hole at the bottom. At sunset, the jar was filled with water, which flowed out at a constant rate. Each mark that appeared as the water dripped out meant that another period of time had passed.

Water clocks spread from Egypt and became common throughout the Mediterranean world. Ktesibios of Alexandria, who lived in the second century B.C., improved on the first water clock. His clock had a float that sat in a jar of

Third century B.C. Egyptian clepsydra, or water clock

water. As water dripped out of a hole in the bottom of the jar, the float moved downward with the water level. With each unit of passing time, a pointer (often a doll-like figure) on top of the float operated a gear mechanism. The mechanism dropped a pebble, sounded a horn, or made another signal to announce the passage of time.

A Roman engineer, Marcus Vitruvius, wrote this description of the clock:

> In this [jar], the float is placed beside a drum that can turn. They are provided with equally spaced teeth, which teeth impinging on one another cause suitable turnings and movements . . . by which statues are moved, obelisks are turned, pebbles or eggs are thrown, trumpets sound.

chapter four

4

ANCIENT CHINA

Chinese brick painting of a person planting fields, made around A.D. 300

China is one of the world's oldest civilizations, and the ancient Chinese developed some well-known technology—especially in agriculture, medicine, and construction. China's first ruling family, the Shang dynasty, reigned from about 1766 to 1122 B.C. During the Shang dynasty, the Chinese began raising silkworms to produce silk for clothing. Later, the Chinese developed acupuncture, a method for treating disease by inserting needles through the skin. The Great Wall of China, a landmark of military technology built to protect China from invaders, was constructed between 221 and 202 B.C. By A.D. 105, the Chinese had developed the papermaking process.

Chinese contributions to machine-building technology are not as well known. China was isolated from the rest of the ancient world for centuries, and the Chinese were not aware of technology developed in the West. So the Chinese came up with their own solutions to common problems. They developed much of the same machinery as other ancient civilizations, often at about the same time.

The ancient Chinese did develop some machine technology long before the rest of the world, however. The Chinese called one of these machines the Wooden Ox or the Gliding Horse. We call it the wheelbarrow.

THE WOODEN OX

The wheelbarrow combines two simple machines: the lever, and the wheel and axle. The platform of the wheelbarrow is the lever. It lifts the load when force is applied to the handles. The wheel acts as the fulcrum, pivoting beneath the load and also allowing the wheelbarrow to roll easily.

Historians don't all agree on the wheelbarrow's origin. Some historians think that a Chinese general, Jugo Liang, invented the wheelbarrow around A.D. 230. Other historians believe that another Chinese inventor developed the wheelbarrow around A.D. 200. (People in Europe didn't develop the wheelbarrow until around A.D. 1200.)

No matter who invented it, the wheelbarrow became an inexpensive, simple, easy-to-maintain machine for transporting food and equipment. With a wheelbarrow, one soldier could transport enough food to supply four soldiers for three months. Wheelbarrows were used to transport rice, vegetables, and other items—including people. Some Chinese wheelbarrows could hold several passengers.

CASTING IRON

Though wrought iron was used first in the ancient Middle East, it was the Chinese who first learned to cast iron.

Modern model of an ancient Chinese wheelbarrow

Metalworkers were able to melt iron and pour it into molds. The Chinese developed the process around 300 B.C., hundreds of years earlier than other civilizations.

Why were the Chinese able to melt iron when other groups could not? Geological factors helped in the process. In China, iron is found in ore that contains large amounts of phosphorus. This ore melts at a lower temperature than ore found in the ancient Middle East, so it is easier to cast. Chinese soil also contains clay that withstands high temperatures. The ancient Chinese used this clay to make furnaces, containers for holding melted iron, and molds for casting it.

The Chinese used cast iron to make tools, weapons, and supports for buildings. People in Europe didn't learn about the Chinese process for casting iron until around A.D. 1310. Until then, Europeans mainly used wrought iron.

Iron hoe (left), and a mold for casting iron (above)

THE BELLOWS

Have you ever blown on the glowing coals of a charcoal fire in a barbecue? The oxygen from your breath makes the fire burn hotter.

You can also use a bellows to blow air and make a fire burn hotter. A bellows is a machine with a chamber, often made from leather, that expands to fill with air. When the air-filled chamber is compressed, air rushes out of an opening at the end of the chamber.

This simple device played an important role in allowing the ancient Chinese to develop technology for casting iron. Sometime between the fourth and third centuries B.C., the Chinese developed a hand-operated bellows that produced very strong currents of air. When blown into a charcoal or coal fire, the airstream provided extra oxygen that would make the fire burn much hotter. The bellows made it easier for Chinese metalworkers to heat furnaces to the temperatures needed to melt iron ore.

Many historians think that sometime around A.D. 30, a Chinese government official named Tu Shih invented the first water-powered bellows. This was a complicated machine containing gears, axles, and levers that was powered by a waterwheel.

Such advanced technology could not have been developed overnight. Engineers think the Chinese must have made simpler water-powered machines long before Tu Shih's water-powered bellows. Though Greek and Roman engineers left written records about building waterwheels, they may not have been the first to make them. The Chinese may have used simple waterwheels centuries earlier.

ANCIENT CYBERNETICS

Have you ever heard of a science called cybernetics? It deals with automatic control systems in machines, in living things, and even in organizations such as businesses. A cybernetic system, such as an autopilot system on an airplane, uses feedback from the environment to control the machine. The word *cybernetics* comes from the Greek *kybernetes*, which means "steersman" or "governor."

A mathematician named Norbert Wiener started the modern science of cybernetics in A.D. 1948. But some people think that the first cybernetic machine was actually developed in ancient China. This machine was a direction

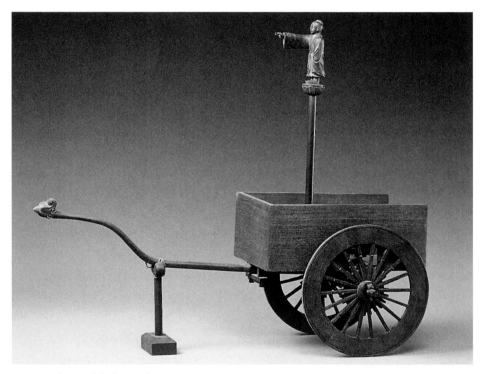

Modern model of a south-pointing carriage

finder called a south-pointing carriage. Some experts believe the Duke of Chou, who lived in China around 1030 B.C., invented the south-pointing carriage. Dr. Joseph Needham, a historian of science, thinks the machine is not that old. More likely, Needham thinks, it was built sometime during the middle of the third century A.D. by a Chinese engineer named Ma Jun.

The south-pointing carriage looked like an ordinary wagon. It was pulled by animals and had ordinary wooden wheels. But the wheels were connected by a series of gears to a jade statue mounted on top of the carriage. No matter which way the carriage turned, the statue always turned in response, so that its arm always pointed south. One Chinese historian described the vehicle:

> The south-pointing carriage was first constructed by the Duke of Chou as a means of conducting homewards certain envoys who had arrived from a great distance beyond the frontiers. The country was a boundless plain in which people lost their bearings as to east and west, so the Duke caused this vehicle to be made in order that the ambassadors should be able to distinguish north and south.

The south-pointing carriage did not contain a magnetic compass, a device that has since become commonly used for determining direction. The statue on top always pointed south because it was connected to the wheels by a series of complex gears known in modern times as differential gears.

Cars have differential gears. When a car turns a corner, the outer and inner wheels must turn at different speeds and travel different distances. The outer wheels have to travel farther than the wheels near the corner. The car's differential system senses the need for different speeds and distances and controls how quickly the wheels turn. A famous historian of science, Professor Derek de Solla Price, called the differential gear "one of the greatest basic mechanical inventions of all time."

Gears in the south-pointing carriage worked much like modern differential gears. They sensed changes in the carriage's direction and provided feedback to other gears that always kept the statue pointing south.

The ancient Greeks usually get credit for inventing differential gears around 30 B.C. But the Chinese invented the south-pointing carriage centuries earlier.

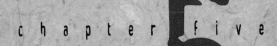

5

ANCIENT GREECE

A sixth century B.C. vase painting showing blacksmiths working at a furnace

The ancient Greeks believed that 12 powerful gods ruled the world from Mount Olympus, a snow-covered peak in northern Greece. In Greek paintings and sculptures, only one of these gods looks dirty and ugly. This was Hephaestus, the god who made machines and other objects from metal.

Why did the ancient Greeks look down on machines? For one thing, Greece was one of the most learned civilizations of the ancient world. It was home to great philosophers, writers, and artists. Concerned mainly with art and philosophy, Greek society didn't much value the study of machines. The Greeks thought engineering was a lowly craft, beneath the dignity of educated people.

Ancient Greece was a very powerful force. Greek soldiers conquered many other regions and made its prisoners of war into slaves. This way the Greeks had plenty of cheap labor. They did not see much need for labor-saving devices. They did value machinery in warfare, but they often viewed other machines as simply toys or amusements.

Despite these attitudes, the ancient Greeks made great contributions to machine technology—especially in the creation of weapons. They produced some of the world's greatest engineers and scientists. Some Greek machinery remained the most advanced in the world for 1,500 years.

THE SCREW

By the time of the ancient Greeks, all the simple machines had been invented but one. The last simple machine was the screw. It was developed in ancient Greece.

The screw is based on another simple machine, the inclined plane. The threads, or ridges, on a screw provide mechanical advantage just as an inclined plane does. Only instead of aiding movement in a straight line, screw threads allow movement in a circular direction.

Screws are often used as fastening devices. You've probably used screws to attach two pieces of wood or metal. Turning the screw provides force that presses the two pieces of material together. Screws are also used to lift loads. For instance, some jacks that lift cars and other heavy objects are actually large screws.

Some experts believe that the brilliant Greek engineer and mathematician Archimedes invented the screw. Others credit an engineer named Archytas of Tarentum with the invention. Archytas lived from 400 to 350 B.C. He made many machines, including a mechanical bird that really flew.

One of the screw's most important uses in ancient times was in the screw press. This device combined two simple

Greek screw press, as depicted on a Roman relief

machines, the screw and the lever, to magnify force. Ancient people used the screw press to squeeze juice and oil from grapes and olives.

Screw presses were large machines. Some of the biggest ones were turned by oxen. Others could be operated by a single person. The screw in the screw press was upright, and turning it put upward pressure on a lever. As one end of the lever moved up, the opposite end moved down, squeezing olives or grapes inside a container. Presses that preceded the screw press used a winch to pull the lever down. But the winch presses yielded less juice and oil.

An inventor named Hero of Alexandria made the screw press even better. His press didn't have a lever. It used the screw to apply force directly to grapes and olives. Less energy was wasted in friction, and the press removed even more grape juice and olive oil.

A GREAT INVENTOR

Hero invented other remarkable machines. One, the aeolipile, was a simple steam engine. Another was a small windmill, used to pump air in a toy organ. Hero apparently didn't care about practical uses for these machines. He simply used his inventions as toys.

He also used weights, strings, and rotating drums to build a miniature theater. It contained mechanical dolls that put on a play. Hero also thought of this invention as a toy to amuse people. Could he have used his mechanical knowledge to make robots that would carry out useful work?

Hero invented a machine that pumped water in a steady

Modern model of Hero's steam engine

stream, much like a modern fire hose. He based this pump and other inventions on discoveries made two hundred years earlier by Ktesibios of Alexandria. The pump used a complicated system of valves, chambers, and pistons to keep the water moving in an unbroken stream.

Unfortunately, Hero's directions for building the pump were lost during the Middle Ages, which began after the fall of the Roman Empire, in A.D. 476. In the early part of the Middle Ages, learning declined and people forgot much of the knowledge of ancient times. It wasn't until the late A.D. 1600s that an engineer finally built a pump that could squirt water as well as Hero's fire hose.

Hero's steam engine was an advanced type, now called a reaction turbine. It had a chamber filled with water, which was heated to produce steam. The steam was fed through tubes into a hollow metal ball. Two more tubes extended from opposite sides of the ball, their ends bent at right angles. As steam hissed out of these tubes, the force of the steam spun the ball. The spinning ball could have been used to power machinery.

Modern engineers have built engines based on Hero's design. They found that the ball rotated fast, at speeds up to 1,500 revolutions per minute. Why didn't Hero put his engine to practical use? Perhaps because the engine rotated too fast. People in ancient Greece would have benefited most from a low-speed engine. It might have been used to grind grain.

Hero wrote at least 13 books, including *Siegecraft*, *Automaton-making*, *Geometrica*, *Pneumatics*, *Mirrors*, and part of a dictionary of technology. One of Hero's most important works was *Mechanics*, a textbook for engineers, architects, and builders. It described the principles behind simple machines and helped people realize that these machines are the basis for all other machines.

THE EINSTEIN OF ANTIQUITY

Many historians of science give that title to Archimedes. Archimedes is perhaps most famous for discovering the principle of buoyancy. That principle explains how an object immersed in water loses weight equal to the weight of the fluid it displaces, or pushes aside. Legend says that Archimedes discovered the principle of displacement while sitting in a bathtub. Thrilled, he ran naked into the street yelling, *"Eureka!"* ("I have found it!").

Archimedes also laid the foundation for calculus, a system of mathematics used in many branches of engineering. Two seventeenth-century mathematicians, Isaac Newton and Gottfried Leibniz, invented calculus. But Archimedes discovered many of its basics, including ways to determine the area and volume of cylinders and spheres.

Archimedes described many mathematical techniques in a book, *The Method*, that was lost during the Middle Ages and rediscovered in the eighteenth century. Some mathematicians suspect that the ancient Greeks kept the book a secret because it contained instructions for building catapults, cranes, and other war machines.

Archimedes also invented machines. Archimedes' screw was a device for pumping water from rivers and irrigation channels. One form of the screw was a hollow shaft with a spiral tube inside. By rotating the shaft with a crank, people could pump water from the bottom of the tube to the top.

Archimedes did not discover the lever. This simple machine had been in use since the Stone Age. But Archimedes discovered the law of the lever, which described the principles behind the lever. The law explained how loads of different weights could be lifted with the same amount of force just by varying the location of the fulcrum.

After discovering the law, Archimedes made a famous statement about the power of levers and other machines: "Give me a place to stand, and I will move the Earth!"

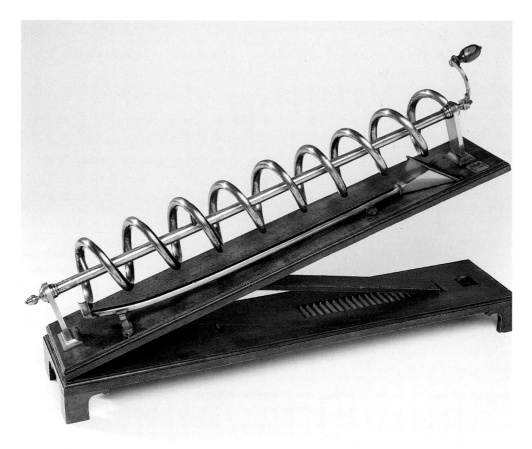

Modern model of Archimedes' screw

Hiero, the King of Syracuse, decided to put Archimedes' boast to a test. He asked Archimedes to single-handedly launch a huge warship from the dry dock where it had been built. The ship was fully loaded with crew and cargo.

Such a job usually required hundreds of strong men pulling on ropes. Archimedes was probably in his 60s. How could he do the job alone? He devised a system of compound pulleys that allowed him to move the ship while sitting comfortably in a chair on the dock. All he had to do was pull on a few ropes!

ANCIENT R&D

Many important advances in technology come from research and development (R&D) programs. In these programs, teams of experts work together to develop products for government or business. The researchers set goals, conduct experiments and tests, and use the results to build the best products.

Thomas Edison, the great American inventor who lived from A.D. 1847 to 1931, is often credited with setting up the first research and development laboratory. Edison's R&D teams developed the electric lightbulb, the phonograph, and other devices.

But many experts believe Dionysius the Elder organized the world's first R&D program in 399 B.C. Dionysius ruled the Greek colony of Syracuse in Sicily. He needed new weapons to prepare Syracuse for war with Carthage, a powerful city-state on the coast of North Africa.

Dionysius assembled large teams of specialists. He broke their tasks into small parts and assigned one part to each team. He gave his researchers cash bonuses for accomplishing their goals on schedule. He frequently reminded researchers that their homeland and the lives of their families and friends depended on the results of their research.

WAR MACHINES

Dionysius's R&D program produced the first true war machines—catapults. These enormous machines shot arrows and rocks much farther and more accurately than any soldier could shoot by hand.

Catapults operated much like handheld bows, only they were many times larger. One was as tall as a telephone pole and rested on a base measuring about eight feet by eight feet. Some could shoot 13-foot arrows and 172-pound stones. Marcus Vitruvius wrote about catapults that could fire stones as heavy as 350 pounds. These would have been real monsters! Nobody knows if they were actually ever built.

The catapult had a big flexible bow mounted on a strong wooden frame. Bows were made of animal horn and tendons and of wood. These were combined for great flexibility. Bowstrings were made of animal tendons and hair and other fibers. Soldiers drew, or flexed, the bow by turning a crank or winch that pulled on the bowstring. They fired the catapult with a trigger mechanism that released the bowstring.

Ancient engineers eventually redesigned catapults, replacing the flexible bow with torsion springs made from animal hair and tendon, twisted up tight by a winch. The newer catapults were far more powerful than the original ones and could hurl arrows and stones much farther.

A German officer in the early A.D. 1900s reconstructed

ancient catapults using Dionysius's original plans. The engineers found these devices to be extremely accurate. One catapult could fire an arrow into a target, split that arrow with the next shot, and fire the next arrow into precisely the same spot.

A NEW IMAGE FOR ENGINEERS

Remember how engineers in ancient Greek society had a bad image? People looked down on them for working with their hands. Creation of the catapult greatly increased the status of engineers, because it took special skills to design, build, aim, and maintain these giant missile launchers.

Greek engineers in the third century B.C. used a complex

Modern illustration of two types of ancient Greek torsion catapults used in siege warfare

formula to design stone-throwing catapults. The formula stated that the diameter of one part of the catapult had to be 1.1 times the cube root of one hundred times the weight of the stone. Finding cube roots involved advanced mathematics.

The Greeks began to appreciate mathematical skills and began to place more value on the engineers that used them. The Greek army needed catapult specialists and created an elite team of soldiers to operate the machines. These specialists had a safer job than ordinary infantrymen. Their work did not involve hand-to-hand combat. They could not be replaced by ordinary soldiers and thus were more valuable. The specialists' importance increased as ancient armies and navies came to depend more on machines than on human muscles.

CHANGING WARFARE

Ancient cities were usually surrounded by large stone walls. During an attack called a siege, an army would surround an enemy city and repeatedly fire on the walls. The attacking army also prevented food, water, and fuel from entering the city. Sometimes starvation caused the besieged city to surrender.

But sieges did not always work quickly. Often they went on for years. For instance, the siege of Troy during the Trojan War lasted for 10 years. With the invention of catapults, though, sieges became more effective. An attacking army could aim its catapults at one area of a city's walls and break through quickly. A military engineer named Philo of Byzantium wrote in 200 B.C. that city walls had to be at least 15 feet thick to withstand catapult stones.

Catapults also brought about the first psychological warfare, in which attacking troops tried to discourage and frighten the enemy. Soldiers aimed their catapults during the day. Then they fired them at night to keep city residents awake and on edge. Sometimes, soldiers turned and ran at the mere sight of an enemy rolling a catapult into firing position.

Catapults also changed naval warfare. Before catapults, naval forces often attacked by ramming the side of an enemy ship and then boarding it. Once on board, soldiers battled with swords and spears in hand-to-hand combat.

Navies armed with catapults fought long-distance battles, however. They no longer rammed and boarded enemy ships. And since the ships did not have to reach high speeds for effective ramming, they needed fewer rowers. Thus warships became smaller. Shipbuilders also began to add layers of armor to protect ships against catapult impacts.

Archimedes' War Machines

Roman sailors attacking the port city of Syracuse in 215 B.C. got a big surprise when they sailed near the city walls. The sailors planned to set big ladders, with rooflike coverings for protection, against the walls and swarm over the top into the city.

The surprise came from Archimedes, who was then serving as military engineer for Syracuse. Archimedes had designed huge cranes, much like modern construction cranes. Rigged with pulleys and powered by oxen, these cranes could lift huge boulders and lead balls, some weighing six hundred pounds. When the Romans approached, crane

Bust of Archimedes, the "Einstein of Antiquity"

operators swung the weights over the city walls and dropped them on the attacking ships, smashing them.

Archimedes made another terrifying weapon—a crane with an enormous, clawlike grappling hook on the end of a rope. Greek soldiers would lower the hook into the water and snag the hull of an approaching Roman ship. Then oxen and pulleys went into action, lifting ships right out of the water. The Greek writer Plutarch, who lived from A.D. 46 to 119, gave this description of the Claws of Archimedes:

The ships, drawn by engines within and whirled about, were dashed against steep rocks that stood jutting out under the walls, with great destruction of the soldiers that were aboard them. A ship was frequently lifted to a great height in the air, a dreadful thing to behold, and was rolled to-and-fro, and kept swinging, until the sailors were all thrown out, when at length it was dashed against the rocks, or was dropped.

Archimedes' war machines were so awesome that Roman ships turned away whenever the Syracusians swung a crane over the city walls.

ANCIENT MACHINE GUNS

The engineer Dionysius of Alexandria developed the first known automatic weapon during the third century B.C. It was a repeating catapult that continually fired arrows from a firing chamber. The arrows fell one after another into the chamber, which was turned by a flat-linked chain. As one arrow fired, another fell into place.

This catapult never replaced single-shot machines because it had a short range—only about six hundred feet as opposed to six hundred yards for ordinary catapults. Officers also disliked the repeating catapult because they thought it encouraged soldiers to waste ammunition. Guess what the biggest objection was to the first automatic rifles, invented two thousand years later? Officers worried that soldiers would waste bullets by firing too often.

CHAINS AND JOINTS

The flat-linked chain used in the repeating catapult was an important advance in machine technology. It resembled a bicycle chain, similar to those still used in many modern machines. Until experts studied ancient catapult designs, they thought Leonardo da Vinci, the Italian engineer who lived from A.D. 1452 to 1519, invented the flat-linked chain. But they have since discovered that the chain originated 1,600 years earlier.

Another modern tool with ancient roots is the universal joint, a linking device that connects two shafts. The joint got its name because it allows movement in all, or universal, directions. Universal joints are used to transmit power when two shafts do not line up exactly. Universal joints are found in many modern machines, including motor vehicle transmissions.

Historians once credited the invention of the universal joint to Robert Hooke, an English scientist who lived from A.D. 1635 to 1703, and to Girolamo Cardano, an Italian mathematician who lived from A.D. 1501 to 1576. But studies of catapult designs show that the universal joint was actually invented at least 1,800 years earlier. Aiming a catapult required a joint that could rotate in almost any direction. The result was a device very similar to the modern universal joint.

GEARS

Gears are toothed wheels that transfer motion from one shaft in a machine to another. Gears can also run a drive chain, such as the chain on a bicycle. Two or more gears can be meshed together to make a gear train.

Gears were developed in ancient times and were in widespread use by the first century A.D. The first gears were wooden wheels with small spokes projecting from the rim. These spokes meshed with spokes in another wheel, so the motion of one wheel could turn another.

Greek engineers were fascinated with gears because they could do more than just transfer motion. They could also change the direction, force, and speed of motion. For example, gears on a driver shaft (the shaft connected to the power source) rotate in the opposite direction of gears on the driven shaft. A small gear turning a larger gear magnifies force. A large gear turning a smaller gear magnifies speed. Gears can be combined into gear trains to achieve various combinations of speed, force, and direction.

Ancient engineers were so intrigued with these combinations that they built elaborate machines with dozens of different gears. Some engineers thought that a weak force could be magnified endlessly through gear trains. They believed that with gear trains, the slightest touch of a finger could lift a heavy load. These engineers did not realize that friction between gears drains away power, so that large numbers of gears lose mechanical advantage.

The world's first known description of gears and gear trains comes from a book with the same name as one of Hero's books—*Mechanics*. It is the oldest known engineering textbook. Some experts believe *Mechanics* was written by the Greek scientist and philosopher Aristotle, who lived from 384 to 322 B.C. Others think the author was an engineer named Straton of Lampskos, who lived during the same period. In addition to describing gears, *Mechanics* includes an early discussion of friction.

THE ANTIKYTHERA MACHINE

One day in A.D. 1900, Greek divers were searching the ocean bottom for natural sponges in the crystal-clear waters off Antikythera, an island north of Crete. There they discovered the wreck of an ancient cargo ship that had sunk two thousand years earlier. The divers brought up many relics, including marble statues and pieces of bronze.

As Greek archaeologists cleaned the bronze, they discovered a series of gear wheels. The gears were precisely made and obviously were the remains of some machine. What was it?

In the A.D. 1950s, the Yale University historian Derek de Solla Price began studying the machine. After years of work, he concluded that it was an advanced astronomical computer from ancient Greece. The device used more than

The Antikythera machine, used to calculate the positions of the sun and the moon

20 gears to calculate the rising and setting of the sun, the moon, and important stars.

Professor de Solla Price built a model and found that the machine looked much like an old-fashioned table clock. It was probably housed inside a wooden case with a door. A person could adjust the machine for a certain day of the year and find out when the sun and other astronomical objects would rise and set.

The Antikythera machine was probably the most advanced computing device of the ancient world. Not until one thousand years later did an Islamic writer named al-Biruni describe a similar machine. His was much simpler.

Professor de Solla Price said that the Antikythera machine showed the ancient Greeks' advanced knowledge of mechanical engineering. "They could have built almost anything they wanted to," he concluded.

ANCIENT ROME

While the ancient Greeks loved knowledge for knowledge's sake and often looked down on machinery, the ancient Romans were just the opposite. They placed great value on machines. Roman engineers used mechanical knowledge to build roads, aqueducts, bridges, mills, and weapons. While Greek mathematicians developed geometry and trigonometry, and admired them for philosophical reasons, Roman engineers put these systems to practical use in their construction projects. Little of what Roman engineers did was original. But the Romans did a good job of improving on technology developed by other ancient cultures.

Though the Romans loved machines, they had one of the same concerns about technology that modern people have. Technology sometimes increases unemployment. Modern factories that use robots and other automation need fewer employees. Roman emperors wanted to keep their people working—to the point that they sometimes discouraged the use of laborsaving technology.

Gaius Tranquillus, a historian who lived from about A.D. 69 to 122, told this story about Emperor Vespasian:

> An engineer offered to haul some huge columns up to the Capitol at moderate expense by a simple mechanical contrivance. But Vespasian declined his services: "I must always ensure," he said, "that the working classes earn enough money to buy themselves food." Nevertheless, he paid the engineer a very handsome fee.

A New Prime Mover

A prime mover is a machine that transforms heat, wind, or flowing water into mechanical energy that can power other machines. A prime mover might rotate a shaft, for instance, which might turn a wheel or gear. Prime movers include waterwheels, windmills, steam engines, internal combustion engines, and jet engines.

New prime movers often have revolutionary effects on society. James Watt's steam engine, for instance, helped bring about the Industrial Revolution of the eighteenth and nineteenth centuries A.D. The internal combustion engine gave people new forms of transportation—automobiles and airplanes. The jet engine increased the speed of travel.

Human muscles were the first prime movers. The domestication of animals, especially oxen around 6500 B.C., gave humans another prime mover. Harnessed animals could turn larger mills and carry heavier loads than humans could. It took almost seven thousand years for people to develop the next prime mover. This was the waterwheel, first used to grind grain.

Modern model of the Greek mill, a horizontal waterwheel

THE GREEK MILL

The first waterwheel, sometimes called the Norse mill or Greek mill, was used in Greece during the first century B.C. It was a wooden wheel with six to eight scoops connected to a shaft. The wheel was placed horizontally (sideways) in a fast-running stream, and it turned with the current. The shaft turned, and large stones connected to it were used to grind grain.

The Greek mill was not very powerful. It took hours to grind one hundred pounds of grain. One expert estimated that the mill produced no more than one-half horsepower, which means it was less powerful than a modern gasoline lawn mower. Two people or a donkey could supply as much power.

THE ROMAN MILL

Roman engineers copied the Greek mill and greatly improved its design. They converted the horizontal waterwheel into the vertical (upright) waterwheel that we sometimes still see.

There are two kinds of vertical waterwheels. The undershot wheel has blades that dip into moving water. As the current pushes the blades, the wheel turns. More efficient is the overshot wheel. It uses a chute to pour water over the top of the wheel. The wheel thus turns with the current and with the weight of the falling water. Water weighs a lot—about eight pounds per gallon—and makes an overshot wheel turn faster than an undershot wheel. The Romans used both kinds of vertical waterwheels.

The ancient Roman mill was a powerful new prime mover. Experts estimate that even the most primitive Roman mill could grind thousands of pounds of grain a day.

The Roman mill is sometimes called the Vitruvian mill, named after its inventor, Marcus Vitruvius. Vitruvius was a Roman engineer and architect who lived in the first century B.C. He worked for the Roman rulers Julius Caesar and Augustus Caesar and was regarded as one of the period's greatest engineers. He wrote a book, *De architectura* "On architecture," that was lost during the Middle Ages and rediscovered in the A.D. 1500s. For centuries afterward, engineers and architects used its plans and designs in the construction of many buildings.

The Vitruvian mill gave Romans the most powerful prime mover in the ancient world. In addition to grinding grain, it could have been used to process fibers and create new products. It could have been the basis of an ancient industrial revolution.

Yet the mill was never used on a wide scale in ancient Rome. Of the three hundred grain mills in the city of

Rome during the third century A.D., only a few were powered by water. Most were powered by slaves. Why not use water power instead? Some experts think that the Romans saw no need for mechanized mills. They had plenty of slaves for cheap labor. People rarely take advantage of technology unless they need it or see its benefits.

AN ANCIENT FACTORY

In the modern town of Barbegal in southern France (which was once part of the Roman Empire), archaeologists have found the remains of an immense Roman flour mill built during the fourth century A.D. The mill gives us a glimpse

Roman stone relief of a donkey-powered grain mill

of how waterwheels might have been able to power large factories in ancient times.

An inscription on a nearby tomb suggests that the mill was built by Quintus Candidius Benignus, a Roman engineer. The inscription praises him for being "clever like none other, and none surpassed him in the construction of machines."

The factory consisted of two parallel rows of eight stone buildings, constructed on the slope of a hill. Each building

Ruins of Roman mills at Barbegal, France; modern model of the Barbegal mills (inset)

was a grain mill with its own waterwheel. Two channels of water ran down the hill, cascading onto the first wheel, then the next and the next. After turning the final wheel, the water ran into a drain and out to a marshy area about a quarter of a mile away.

Archaeologists estimate that these 16 waterwheels produced enough power to grind about 9,900 pounds of flour each day. That flour could have fed about 12,500 people. The mill probably produced flour for the nearby city of Arles, which had a population of about 12,000 at the time.

The ancient factory probably produced no more than 30 horsepower, equal to about six modern lawn mowers. But experts believe that it had the greatest concentration of mechanical power in Europe. It wasn't until the development of the steam engine, centuries later, that any place in Europe produced more power.

THE END OF ANCIENT TIMES

Ancient times ended when the Western Roman Empire fell in A.D. 476. Barbarians invaded Rome from the north, and the Middle Ages began. Progress in machine technology as well as other kinds of technology stopped. Many important machines were forgotten. These included Hero's steam engine, Vitruvius's engineering designs, and the differential gears in the south-pointing carriage.

When rediscovered centuries later, ancient machines helped lead to the modern machine age with its internal combustion engines, industrial robots, and space shuttles. These inventions were all based on the six simple machines and the work of the great ancient engineers.

GLOSSARY

cast—to create objects by pouring melted metal into molds for hardening

differential gears—a system of gears that allow different parts of a machine to move at different speeds

force—physical effort that causes an object to move or stop moving

friction—the force that acts against motion when one surface rubs against another

fulcrum—the support or pivot point about which a lever turns in raising or moving an object

inclined plane—a ramp or other angled surface that allows people to lift objects using less force

lever—a beam or bar that allows people to move objects or lift loads

machine—a device that performs work by increasing or changing the direction of force

mechanical advantage—the degree to which a machine increases force

prime mover—a machine, such as a steam engine or waterwheel, that provides energy to power another machine

pulley—a grooved wheel attached to a rope. Pulleys allow people to change the direction of force when lifting a load.

screw—a rod surrounded by a spiral ridge that works like an inclined plane. Screws are used to fasten and lift objects.

wedge—a piece of metal or wood that is thicker at one end than at the other. Wedges are used to move objects short distances.

wheel and axle—a combination of two wheels of different sizes. The wheel and axle is used to increase or reduce force.

work—the amount of energy needed to move an object over a particular distance

Selected Bibliography

Bruno, Leonard C. *The Tradition of Technology: Landmarks of Western Technology.* Washington, D.C.: Library of Congress, 1995.

Bunch, Bryan, and Alexander Hellemans. *The Timetables of Technology.* New York: Simon & Schuster, 1993.

Clark, Ronald W. *Works of Man: A History of Invention and Engineering, from the Pyramids to the Space Shuttle.* New York: Viking, 1985.

De Camp, L. Sprague. *The Ancient Engineers.* New York: Ballantine, 1974.

Gonen, Rivka. *Charge! Weapons and Warfare in Ancient Times.* Minneapolis: Runestone Press, 1993.

Hackett, General Sir John. *Warfare in the Ancient World.* New York: Facts on File, 1989.

Hill, Donald. *A History of Engineering in Classical and Medieval Times.* London: Routledge, 1996.

Mason, Antony. *The Children's Atlas of Civilizations.* Brookfield, Conn.: Millbrook, 1994.

St. John, Jeffrey, and the editors of Time-Life Books. *Noble Metals (Planet Earth).* Alexandria, Virg.: Time-Life Books, 1984.

Scarre, Chris. *Smithsonian Timelines of the Ancient World: A Visual Chronology from the Origins of Life to A.D. 1500.* London: Dorling Kindersley, 1993.

Schick, Kathy D., and Nicholas Toth. *Making Silent Stones Speak: Human Evolution and the Dawn of Technology.* New York: Simon & Schuster, 1993.

Schiller, Ronald. *Distant Secrets: Unravelling the Mysteries of Our Ancient Past.* New York: Carol Publishing, 1989.

Soedel, Werner, and Vernard Foley. "Ancient Catapults." *Scientific American* (March 1979): 150-160.

Waechter, John. *Man before History: The Making of the Past.* New York: Dutton, 1976.

Williams, Trevor I. *The History of Invention.* New York: Facts on File, 1987.

INDEX

Note: There are alternate spellings for some of the names mentioned in this book. Here are a few examples:
Ktesibios or Ctesibius (Egypt)
Herodotus or Herodotos (Egypt)
Chou or Zhou (China)
Ramses or Ramesses or Rameses (Egypt)
Khufu or Cheops (Egypt)

About the Authors

Michael Woods is an award-winning science and medical writer with the Washington bureau of the *Toledo Blade* and the *Pittsburgh Post Gazette.* His articles and weekly health column, "The Medical Journal," appear in newspapers around the United States. Born in Dunkirk, New York, Mr. Woods developed a love for science and writing in childhood and studied both topics in school. His many awards include an honorary doctorate degree for helping to develop the profession of science writing. His previous work includes a children's book on Antarctica, where he has traveled on three expeditions.

Mary B. Woods is an elementary school librarian in the Fairfax County, Virginia, public school system. Born in New Rochelle, New York, Mrs. Woods studied history in college and later received a master's degree in library science. She is coauthor of a children's book on new discoveries about the ancient Maya civilization.

Photo acknowledgments: The photographs in this book are reproduced courtesy of Bridgeman Art Library, London/New York: (Ashmolean Museum, Oxford, UK) p. 1, (Louvre, Paris, France) pp. 19, 20-21; Art Resource: (Erich Lessing) pp. 2-3, 11, 12-13, 76-77, (Scala) p. 59; Canadian Museum of Civilization, p. 15; National Museums of Canada, p.17; Laura Westlund, p. 23; Michael C. Carlos Museum of Emory University, p. 26; Wilford Archaeology Laboratory, University of Minnesota, p. 28; © Ronald Sheridan/Ancient Art & Architecture Collection, Ltd., pp. 31, 34-35, 56-57; John Kreul, p. 33; Oriental Institute of The University of Chicago, pp. 38, 43; The Illustrated London News, pp. 40-41; ChinaStock: (© Christopher Liu) pp. 45, 49, 50 (upper and lower), 52, (© Ru Suichu) pp. 46-47; © C. M. Dixon, p. 55; Dorling Kindersley, pp. 60, 79; Science Museum/Science & Society Picture Library, pp. 63, 69; North Wind Picture Archives, p. 66; Laurie Platt Winfrey, Inc., p. 73; E.T. Archive, p. 75; The Granger Collection, p. 81; © Tor Eigeland, p. 82 (both).

Front cover photographs courtesy of: Science Museum/Science & Society Picture Library (left), Laurie Platt Winfrey, Inc. (right)
Back cover photograph courtesy of: Canadian Museum of Civilization